A LOVE STORY WAITING TO HAPPEN
CRYSTAL C. MERCER

A LOVE STORY WAITING TO HAPPEN

CRYSTAL C. MERCER

Copyright © 2017 The Butterfly Typeface Publishing

Cover Formatting © 2017 Ministering Moments Photography
Cover Design © 2017 Crystal C. Mercer
Cover Photo and Photo Credits © 2017 Joshua Asante.
All rights reserved.

All rights reserved. No part of this book maybe reproduced in any form or by any electronic or mechanical means – except in the case of brief quotations embodied in articles or reviews – without written permission from its publisher.

All Poems Copyright © 2017 Crystal C. Mercer
All rights reserved.

ISBN 9781947656161
ISBN10 1947656163

Butterfly Typeface Publishing
P.O. Box 56193
Little Rock, AR 72215
www.butterflytypeface.com
info@butterflytypeface.com
(501) 823 - 0574

ACKNOWLEDGEMENTS

The moon is not far enough to describe how much I love you... my love is as infinite and ever expanding, like the Universe, for you.

FOR CLAUDIA GISELE AND BIANCA ELISE

MY DEEPEST THANKS

Thank Goddess for you and your divine belief that my words can be a healing balm, a calming song, a declaration for someone's soul.

TO SONTA JEAN AND IRIS WILLIAMS

ROOTS AND LEGACIES

I am, and continue to be, because you are and you made me.

FOR FAMILY: PAST, PRESENT AND FUTURE

TABLE OF CONTENTS

FOREWORD
15 KESHA L. LAGNIAPPE

INTRODUCTION
17 VERDA DAVENPORT-BOOHER

ABOUT THE PHOTOGRAPHY
19 CRYSTAL C. MERCER

EBB
22 DON'T TELL (ME)
23 TODAY'S MANTRA/PRAYER
25 THERE ARE DIFFERENT WAYS TO MAKE LOVE
27 PRAISE GODDESS
29 A PRAYER

FLOW
32 HEARTSTRINGS
34 LOVE IS MAGIC
36 STORYTELLER
38 SUNBATHING

TABLE OF CONTENTS CONTINUED

DISRUPTION
- 40 BLACK MAN/BROKEN HEART
- 42 NO ALLEGIANCE
- 46 JIVE TURKEYS
- 50 THE TEMPLE OF CHURCH
- 54 THE VILLAGE
- 58 YES, I'M MAD AS HELL
- 61 FACT CHECKER

CHAOS
- 67 OPOSSUM
- 68 WAS
- 70 LET THEM EAT CAKE
- 72 TO MY EX(x)
- 73 THE MORNING AFTER
- 76 THE MAN I CAN'T TASTE
- 78 ONCE AGAIN
- 79 YOUR HONEY AIN'T SWEET
- 81 SHOULDA, COULDA, WOULDA
- 85 NOW THAT I HAVE YOUR ATTENTION (THE LAST SAD POEM I WILL WRITE ABOUT YOU/POOF/HE GONE)

TABLE OF CONTENTS CONTINUED

CALM
88 MISCARRIAGE
89 A QUILTED COOL OF CONNECTION
91 HIDE AND SEEK
92 QUESTION
95 AN EVENING IN MISSOULA
96 YOU

GOOD
100 APEX
101 BOULDER OF STRENGTH FOR THE FALLEN
104 TREVIÑO LULLABY
105 I WILL SPEAK YOUR NAME, YOU WILL NEVER DIE

BAD
108 BLESSED BE
109 ALLEY OF WIND
111 FIRE DANCES WITH THE MOON
114 I AM MY OWN MOTHER NOW
116 ?
117 THE WINTER OF MY DISCONTENT
119 CONDOMS AND DAMNATION

TABLE OF CONTENTS CONTINUED

UGLY
124 TIME IS A BIRD
127 SEEDS AND WHATNOTS
129 ONCE UPON A TIME
130 HIM
132 REMINDING MYSELF THAT IT TAKES TIME
134 IN AND OUT OF LOVE
135 (DIS)CARD

LOVELY
138 YOU DON'T WANT TO FALL IN LOVE WITH ME
143 THAT TIME: A LETTER TO MY WOMB
147 I. AM. PERIOD. A WORKING LIST
149 SUGAR
151 FRIDA'S INSTRUCTIONS
153 BLACK LOVE

ABOUT THE BOOK
156 A LOVE STORY WAITING TO HAPPEN

ABOUT THE AUTHOR
157 CRYSTAL C. MERCER

TABLE OF CONTENTS CONTINUED

PHOTO INDEX
159 COVER TO COVER REFLECTIONS OF THE PHOTOGRAPHY

PUBLISHER'S PAGE
165 THE BUTTERFLY TYPEFACE PUBLISHING

FOREWORD
KESHA L. LAGNIAPPE

Stunning. Graceful. Elegant. Even haunting. Living and growing in a world where your skin color is hated, your culture is demeaned to nothing more than a caricature, your features are taught to be unattractive, and every experience you have ever had is invalidated, dismissed, and disregarded, to love yourself and heal is an act of revolution. That is what Crystal C. Mercer's words are: revolutionary. She is a masterful word-architect who builds up heartbreak and trauma only to destroy it all with the amazing power of self-love and freedom. Each letter creates a riot. It will propel you to act. It will bring you to tears. Mercer composes and addresses everything we all feel that we can never find the words for. Her words provide a voice and a battle cry for many that have suffered any type of oppression.

Crystal Colleen Mercer was born and evolved in Little Rock, Arkansas. She is the daughter and namesake of the late Civil Rights Attorney, Christopher Columbus Mercer, Jr. (C.C.). She has dedicated her life not only honoring the legacy of her father and continuing his work, but to serving others. She is a multi-dimensional artist and has endless means and skills to express however she feels at the moment, whether it's acting, poetry, or fiber, and she has a boundless background in theatre as an actor and director. Her work also reflects her life and how it relates to harmful social constructs that oppress and harm her, and others like her, in America and globally. It is a demand for change, revolution, and respect.

INTRODUCTION
VERDA DAVENPORT-BOOHER

"Truth is a spell that should be cast everyday," I don't know when Crystal first wrote these words, but I know that every day, she lives them. The first time I met her, I remember feeling a powerful vibration of recognition, a shadow of consciousness. It took me a while to understand. C.C. offers up her soul, her joy, and her pain in every moment. That is her magic. She is a presence that oozes universal power with a connection to source that I'm not sure even she truly understands. At once free and vulnerable, Crystal has gifted us all a seat right in the sacred space of her soul.

A Love Story Waiting to Happen exposes the radical work of healing. Crystal lays bare her soft places while claiming peace and justice with unyielding power and the grace of a spiritual practice.

ABOUT THE PHOTOGRAPHY
CRYSTAL C. MERCER

Joshua Asante, a noted musician, artist, creator, and photographer is a vortex of Black love and reflection. Asante has been photographing my image and my essence for nearly five years. A month before our first session, September 2013, I turned 30 years old. I had chopped off my signature gigantic Afro into a baby Afro, and I was in a transitional time in my life.

The way Asante shoots is more than clicking camera button; his lens captures the heart and soul of a person. We became friends, and over the years, our sessions became collaborations. Sometimes he had ideas for a shoot or something he wanted to try: be it light, or color, or something ornate. Sometimes I booked him specifically for a vision that I knew only he could see and pull from my headspace into realization.

Paired with my poetry, Asante's photography is a pairing that is parallel with the vision I had for my first full body of work. There are so many waves that have crashed into me, so many waves that have washed my broken, beautiful body ashore, so many waves that have rocked my spirit, and so many waves that have cleansed me anew. Asante has capture most of those moments in my life.

EBB.

Ebb is a stillness that cannot be explained... a pool of quitness.

DON'T TELL (ME)

I know how to keep a secret,
I am a secret,
And I've kept myself for all these years...

TODAY'S MANTRA/PRAYER

If my mind is strong, my body will follow.

My body is beautiful and able.

Truth is a spell that should be cast everyday.

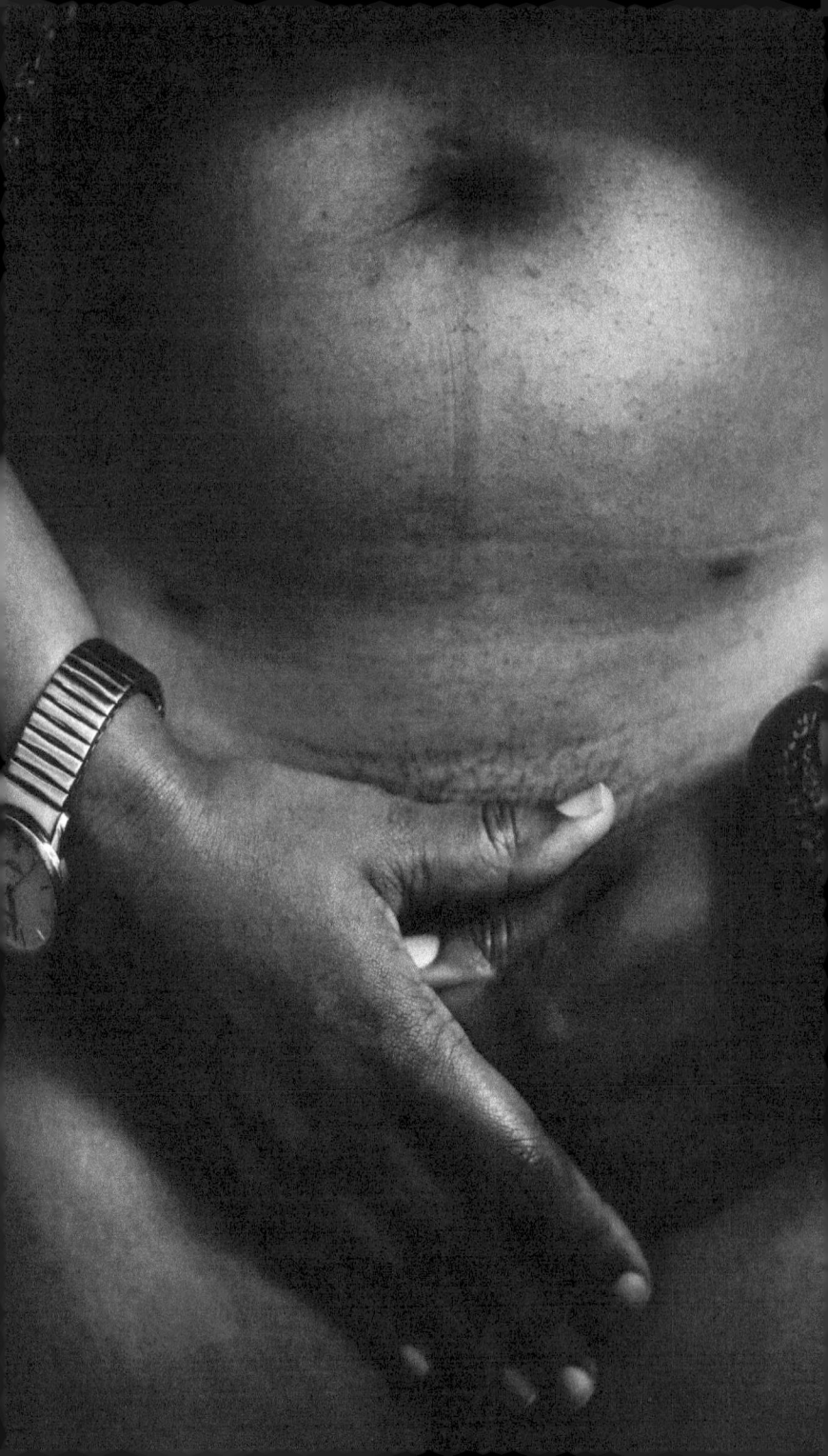

THERE ARE DIFFERENT WAYS TO MAKE LOVE

Where is that quiet place,
I ask myself,
Where I can go,
And remain what I have become,
Where I am more becoming,
Of who I am becoming,
Ever coming,
Into myself,
Without interruption,
Without the noise of the world,
Or the noise I create,
Static of doubt not allowed,
In my quiet space,
In my sacred space,
I run my hands over my scars,
I run my hands over my heart,
It's the only compass I own,
It gives me direction of where to go,
It leads me to my quiet place,
It never lies,
Sometimes she cries,
For her memories,
She remembers everything,
And she knows,

How peace can be still,
How still can be pain,
Stuck,
Frozen,
Hard,
Be soft,
I tell her,
Be humble,
Be wild,
Be certain,
Be spontaneous,
Be free,
Follow yourself,
And I'll follow you,
To that quiet place,
I'll lay there,
I need to Kuti,
Afrobeat my own drum,
Come into my own understanding,
Make love to myself,
I'm glorious,
And free,
Like water,
I flow,
And pool into my quietness.

PRAISE GODDESS

Goddess. Shell. Heaven. Hell.

A PRAYER

A morning prayer,
To the Goddess within,
To her hair and her skin,
And her long lost kin,
To her eyes,
To her thighs,
Thank the red beans and rice,
To her toes,
To her nose,
To her African clothes,
A evening prayer,
To the Goddess within,
To her oils,
To her toils,
And her long lost men,
To her arms,
To her charms,
Thank high heavens she was born,
To her legs,
To her knees,
Black Pyramids and honey bees,

A goodnight prayer,
To the Goddess within,
To her back,
To her hips,
And her long lost kids,
To her hair,
To her glare,
Thank Goddess for her stare,
To her star,
To her power,
To her offerings made on every hour,
Blessed be,
To the Goddess within,
Filled with peace,
Her heart is again,
A daily mantra,
A daily prayer,
To the Goddess that expands my lungs with air.

FLOW.

Flow is fluid and cool; it washes over rocks and makes them smooth, rounded stones.

HEARTSTRINGS

He pulled on that place,
Until she was not herself,
Bending and breaking.

LOVE IS MAGIC

Love is magic,
Dear heart,
If only you believe,
Wear your love on your sleeve,
And eat three cloves for breakfast,
Sage your soul,
With the intent of making,
Love work,
That is your goal,
Love is magic,
Magic that is exists,
Warm,
In a world so cold,
In a heart so old,
Tattered from the rugged storms,
Hear me,
Love is,
Magic,
Dear heart,
In only you believe,
Wear your love on your sleeve,
And drink three rums for lunch,
Burn your oil,
With the intent of making,
Love work,
Open yourself up,
Touch yourself,

On your heart,
Feel what pumping feels like,
What blood does when it bleeds,
I would bleed for you,
But I can't believe for you,
Only tell you,
What I know,
Love is magic,
Dear heart,
If only you believe,
Wear your love on your sleeve,
And eat three moons for dinner,
Say your prayers,
With the intent of making,
Love work,
It does,
Trust me,
I'm magic.

STORYTELLER

There's something behind her eyes,
Stories unfold,
And yet to be told,
Sitting in the sockets of her spheres,
She stands in her favorite mirror,
Says hello to herself,
Admires her beauty,
And makes ready her soul,
For the stories left to tell...

SUNBATHING

The light of the sun on my back,
The green grass between the crack,
Of my toes,
The bees buzzing about my crown,
They must think I'm a flower,
They are correct,
Lavender and rosemary dance in the wind,
Birds singing so sweetly to me,
Beauty is so enchanting,
And it's all around me,
Daffodils in full bloom,
Dogs barking,
Cats crossing the road,
My neighborhood is magical,
All I have to do is step on my porch,
Bathe in the sun,
Take in the Earth in all her glory,
I won't be here for long,
I've got other places to go,
Converse with my father,
Ride a comet clear into outer space,
Drink water on Mars,
Soon,
The sun will greet me closer,
I will ascend,
I will transcend time,
And hopefully I will remember when his rays,
Gently rested on my should blades,
I am certain I will remember him,
This day is too good to forget...

DISRUPTION.

Disruption is a monster with eight heads, a long, jagged back, and a clubbed tail that attempted to block my path.

BLACK MAN / BROKEN HEART

Breaking hearts with bullets,
Shells hit the dirt,
Bodies fall hard,
Black man dead,
Everywhere,
Open season,
For no reason,
He is the target,
Practice,
No patience,
No questions,
Kill him,
Him dead,
Dead and gone
Metal pierces his flesh,
Blood splatters,
Warm,
Thick,
It runs from his wounds,
His screams are ignored,
He dies alone,
On dark streets without names,
At Family Dollar stores in bright day,
On his bicycle while at play,
In front of his family,
Why are we not angry,
Black man is murdered,
America's daily bread,
A treat with her coffee,
A pat on her back,
While he lays in his blood,
Wailing for help,
And nobody comes...

NO ALLEGIANCE

I do not pledge allegiance to any flag,
That drapes bodies bagged and bloodied from war,
Martyrs of barren deserts,
Blasted and fused with the stench of sand and flesh,
Buried under boulders of oppression,
Murderer of my contemporaries,
Dying too soon,
Wounds bleed out,
Organs shut down,
Never will they breathe again,
On their native grounds,
No, I do not pledge that,
Allegiance,
Saluting atmosphere,
As the disturbed leaps from bridges,
Either off to war or out of work,
In a land that boasts of milk and honey,
Endless money,
Freedom for all,
Soldiers can't see once their skulls collide with Earth,
Brains splatter on the pavement,
Hope and life is lost,
And so are we,
Pledging anything to any flag to forces the will of freedom,
No,
I do not pledge allegiance to any flag,
That considers color less than human,
Denies basic liberties from sea to shining sea,
Taxes highly the tired and poor,
To pay for war,
Instead of education,

I do not value any nation that does not value me,
Value humanity,
Creatures,
The planet that curves around our feet,
Gravity has been stripped,
Of those who rip,
Our pride,
Paste our mouths shut with Stars and Stripes,
Forever we fight,
Instead of rally for peace,
And this flag expects us,
To stand to our feet,
Raise our right hand,
Repeat the words,
Repeat the words,
Repeat the words,
Repeat the words,
Until we are comfortable,
Being drones of destruction,
Key keepers to our own cells,
Jailed in our minds,
Condemners of our hearts,
Blinded from the truth,
We walk,
United,
Standing tall,
Leaning on each other,
For we have ripped out our souls,
Gauged out our eyes,
Walk in circles,
Until we meet death,
And accept it all while pledging to some flag,
No,
I will not do that,

No,
I do not pledge my allegiance to any piece of cloth that waves,
Cowards instead of being brave,
Obliterating innocence globally,
Destroying cities in the name of democracy,
Oh beautiful,
For goodness sake,
You can keep your amber waves of grain,
Give me liberty,
Or give me death,
Both choices guarantee my freedom,
But I say again,
Repeat my own words,
Chanel my heart,
And open my eyes,
I'm not falling your lies,
No,
Therefore,
I do not pledge allegiance to any flag,
There are no anthems I would sing,
Unless allegiance is pledged to peace.

JIVE TURKEYS

In this so-called America,
Why are the only consolations for being Black,
Are being slayed into martyrdom,
Or becoming a hashtag,
Hashtag body bag,
Hashtag "Justice For",
When "Justice for one",
Should be "Justice for all",
United we stand,
Divided we fall,
Now it's just us,
Dealing with injustice,
Protesting for a peace that never comes,
Only police with loaded guns,
While we singing "We shall overcome",
But that day never comes,
In America,
Manumission papers burned,
While the Black body churns,
And chokes,
From a popular tree,
Feet never hit the ground,
This is the Miseducation of Mike Brown,
This is the Miseducation of every Black and Brown child,
This is the misappropriation of funds,
America can blow up cities,
But never blow our minds,
Schooling is a waste of time for the fool,
Unless the fool can shoot,
Unless the fool can loot,
And by loot,

In a few weeks when an Anglo is pictured,
The headline will read,
"Searching for food",
I'm ever searching for good,
But the door is always closed,
Hope doesn't float,
But Black bodies did,
When the levees broke,
Black bodies did while in the Middle Passage,
They were "property" in tow,
But how can one properly tow,
The Soul of Black folks,
They must've forgot,
We like to let our Soul Glo,
Coming to America,
In rusty chains,
Surrounded by vomit and piss,
Separated from our mothers,
Castrated from our fathers,
We have no connection to our roots,
Only knots of Bantu,
Kente cloth stitched to white shoes,
A cardboard box,
And a boom box,
Breaking,
Pop and lock,
On the one,
2-3-4-5-6,
Section 8,
Rope chains and tall gates,
Small windows in the project bathrooms,
So we can't see the outside world to dream,
Unless it's hoop dreams,
Rooting for our favorite teams,

Music loud,
Radio Raheem,
Radio the police,
Tell them "I can't breathe",
This is Eric Garner to Radio Raheem,
Brothers from a different time,
But on the same path,
Racism,
That is the song that never ends,
Jim Crow singing like the rent due,
Singing,
I'm gonna get you, Sucka,
But we ain't no suckers,
We are Kings,
Queens,
Divine energy,
Crafted by the hand of God,
Nothing odd about being Black,
In the beginning there was darkness,
Now let there be enlightenment,
Wake up,
And stay woke.

THE TEMPLE OF CHURCH

We are not targets,
We are not catchers of stray,
Or intentional,
Bullets,
While our hands are clasped in prayer,
How dare you separate our bodies from our souls without permission,
This is not the work of God,
This is not the will of the divine,
This is the work of man,
Who understands not his purpose for being,
Bombs over Birmingham,
Jaws ripped open in Memphis on balconies,
Daddies gun downed in their carports,
Brothers wearing X's murdered in front of their own,
Any violent crime,
Doesn't matter the date or time,
The fate of people have been doomed,
Since 1619,
When a ship docked in South Carolina,
Harboring precious cargo,
No stowaways,
Just Negroes,
Before they were Negroes,
Before they were Colored,
Before they were Black,
Before they were African-American,
With or without hyphens,
They were just niggers on a boat,
Beasts not seen as human,
Signed into 3/5 of nothingness on a land that they would build,

However we know,
With praying hands lifted to Ra,
The truth and origin of our intelligence,
Who built the pyramids,
Who irrigated the longest river in the world,
Who grew squash, grains, yams, and indigo,
Who harvested diamonds,
Who documented in glyphs how daily life was lived,
Who could account for every star in the sky,
Black as the night that covers me,
And Black like my people be,
It was us,
So know that we are not targets,
We are not catchers of stray,
Or intentional,
Bullets,
While our hands are clasped in prayer,
How dare you separate our bodies from our souls without permission,
This is not the work of God,
This is not the will of the divine,
This is the work of man,
Who understands not his purpose for being,
They killed our sons,
They killed our husbands,
The streets ran red,
Our daughters cried,
Our mothers died,
Singing for freedom,
We asked,
When will it come,

Mother Emanuel,
Hold your children close,
Even those that have been separated from their souls,
While we wait for change that doesn't rattle in collection plates,
Or brown soldiers we find tossed on the ground faced down...
Real change,
Real change,
Real change,
Tangible and intangible change,
That will uplift the weary,
And free the spirit of Blackness.

THE VILLAGE

Gentrification is the new genocide...
Cyanide with white lines,
For bike lanes,
And pedestrian crossing signs,
New construction,
Old houses torn down,
Historic brick and mortar hit the ground,
Families are forced to move out,
But where to they go?
What happens when some sell out,
Instead of deciding to own?
What happens when we don't have our own?
Where have all the cowboys gone?
Probably drinking themselves under a bridge,
For they have no where to live,
So drink up your Starbucks in your fancy cups,
Nothing like a sip of Black Death to start the day,
Diluted with cream,
And a spoonful of sugar helps the medicine go down,
Downtown,
South and East of what's Central to,
The Village,
Named and mapped out,
New neighborhood signs by the trap house,
Granny's daffodils in bloom,
While the gentrifiers grab their brooms,
And "clean up",
What they see as a dump,
Not respecting the beauty that is,
Not respecting the neighborhood kids,
Who grew up on these blocks,

Played until our mama's called our names,
Or until the street lights came on,
Made the mailbox on the curb home base,
The basketball goal in the yard, second,
The porch was third,
And it rang true,
Kickball,
Baseball,
Any game would do,
But it was home,
Not zoned for takeover,
And rich saviors,
Wealthy friends doing their wealthy friends favors,
But this is our block,
Where auntie and uncle sit,
On their stoops with lemonade they sip,
This ain't no zombie apocalypse,
Black bodies with no brains,
No Scarecrows,
We have diplomas,
You know,
We have heart,
And courage to last our whole lives through,
We have the power to rid ourselves of feuds,
And greed,
We cut our grass,
No weeds,
We water our plants,
All seeds,
All power to all people,
Yes indeed,
So don't be renaming our streets,
To read,
"This is a neighborhood of" so and so division,
Only to create division,

Seems like their math is bad,
To be on the come up,
You gotta add,
Not subtract,
See what I mean?
Gentrification is the new genocide,
Cyanide with white lines,
For bike lanes,
And pedestrian crossing signs,
New construction,
Old houses torn down,
Historic brick and mortar hit the ground,
Families are forced to move out,
But where to they go?
What happens when some sell out,
Instead of deciding to own?
What happens when we don't have our own?
Where have all the cowboys gone?
Probably drinking themselves under a bridge,
For they have no where to live,
So drink up your Starbucks in your fancy cups,
Nothing like a sip of Black Death to start the day...
But we don't die,
We multiply,
Don't believe me,
Just watch and open your eyes,
I will build towers,
I will build nations,
My womb is the Universe,
And it's time to take this city to school,
Class is in session,
Black Power is the lesson,
And the revolution is coming,
To a city near you.

YES, I'M MAD AS HELL

Dear Ms. So-Called America,
With your burning crosses and your flashing blue lights,
You don't have permission to kill,
Our husbands, our sons, our brothers,
Screaming,
"Don't shoot",
With their hands up,
Gasping,
"I can't breathe",
And for the life of me,
You steal the lives of our men,
Dear Ms. So-Called America,
Please tell me when justice will prevail,
Before coffins are purchased for 12 year old boys,
Before Emmett is the only image,
Of our children,
Mothers wailing,
Fathers falling to their knees,
While a sty of pigs,
Laugh in a haze of cigar smoke filled rooms,
Proud of their work,
Feet clicking on the pavement to see another day,
While our babies feet are stuffed into graves,
Dear Ms. So-Called America,
With your double standards,
And biased news,
Your patrol officers are patty rollers in blue,
Beating the hope out of our Blackness,
Killing our seeds,

Making shallow our roots,
And without roots,
We don't grow,
We die,
And you, Ms. So-Called America,
Must believe that it's alright to commitment genocide,
Exterminating Black people like a pastime,
From Biloxi to Bed-sty,
This must be what it sounds like when doves cry,
Every time a Black man dies,
So yes,
I'm mad as hell,
Be it death or be it jail,
You don't have permission to kill
Our husbands, our sons, our brothers,
Walking on eggshells to escape The Reaper,
Cloaked in stars and strips forever,
A bald eagle perched like a crow upon your shoulder,
Black boys die younger,
Never get older,
Snatched from their innocence to drown in pools of blood,
Dear Ms. So-Called America,
Clearly you don't know who we are,
You can kill our dreamers,
But you can't our dreams,
We will still make love to our husbands,
We will still give birth to our babies,
We will still be sisters to our brothers,
Know this, Ms. So-Called America,
We are not pawns,
We are Black,
In the beginning there was darkness,
We have always been here,
And here we will remain.

FACT CHECKER

You can't deify,
And vilify,
My Blackness in the same breath,
Interact with me when it suits you,
Or cloaks you,
In white robes,
Topped with pyramided hoods,
You know we built pyramids in our hoods,
For our Pharaohs,
Aligned with the stars,
Walking round Earth saying that we're not smart,
That those "facts" are "scientific",
Well,
I have got some alternative-actual facts,
If'n you'll listen,
Pangea,
"All Earth",
Our mother,
Broken into pieces,
Africa,
Still Mother,
Giver of life,
Yours and mine,
Lucy revealed herself in 1974,
While Mother Angela was rocking her Fro,
While Fela Kuti gave us Afrobeats,
And The Shrine to move our feet,
All hail to true Kings and Queens,
Repping for their culture,
Ever repping,
Even among vultures,
Who say they love you,
Just to pluck you,
From your shores,

Consume your Black body for coins,
Discard your Black body for sport,
Trade your Black body for processed goods,
Sell your Black body for cotton, cattle, and wood,
You can't praise my color,
Then curse my name,
You can't boast of comfort,
Then leave me cold,
Naked,
Lying on the floor,
With your semen and your sweat diluting with my blood,
Enough,
Stop patronizing me and colonizing me,
My diamonds,
Nor my yams,
Are not for sell,
My Black Pyramid is not for your Heaven or your Hell,
My melons can't be touched,
I swear,
Neither can you touch my hair,
It's my permanent crown,
Curly coif connected to my Colored scalp,
Full of wonder,
Mystery,
Flare,
So don't you dare make me your Goddess then destroy me,
Despise my heart,
Kill my men,
Lie on my sons,
Shoot them on site,
Then lull yourself to sleep with rap lyrics at night,
Demonize our griots,
Poets,
Songs,
Melodies,
Rhythms that always find their way between your ears,
The soundtrack of the Diaspora,

The moans and the wailing,
The tears that thudded against the planks,
Sounds of Blackness,
Against Black skin cracked by the White whip,
Nothing cool about it,
Just facts,
Actual facts,
The facts of how life began in this so-called America,
The facts on how I transcend this so-called America,
I channel my Roots,
Uncle Alex was that dude,
Friends with my father in the bluff of pines,
Giants,
Breakers of chains,
So I'm not going back to a time where I would have been caged,
I know why the caged bird sings,
But I also know she would prefer to spread her wings,
Take flight,
Just a little girl from Little Rock,
Flight Time,
Porters' pulling our heavy load,
Brantons' and Hunts' integrating our graduate schools,
Mercers' making moves,
This is what we do,
My people,
Black people,
"All power to all people",
Black panthers,
Poached for feeding breakfast to their kids,
I am not the enemy,
So stop making me,
A target,
For your shooting range and your shooting games,
I don't wanna play,
I just wanna enjoy my freedom,
Without the two-faces of fools,
I just wanna enjoy my Blackness,
In the corridors of my school,

I just wanna be the CC I was meant to be,
Without the lead blanket of oppression hovering,
Over my back,
Miss me with that,
And those pseudo-compliments,
"She's pretty... for a Black girl",
Bih, recognize a gorgeous Goddess when you see one,
Black Goddess,
Still mother,
Welcome back, Carter,
Times two,
The most radical thing you can do is be yourself,
And have Black babies,
Procreate,
Cause I'm creative,
Creator of Color,
I brighten this world with my smile,
And my child,
Stay tuned,
When my womb heals,
More Black babies coming to a city near you real soon,
I am a Queen,
Not a coon.
Check it.

CHAOS.

Chaos was my lover; what seemed exciting was only a disguise for destruction.

OPOSSUM

I learned how to play dead,
Be quiet and still when you were on the phone with her,
We were having dinner,
We had argued too many times before,
So I sat there,
Quiet,
Forcing food down my throat,
To avoid saying a word to you,
Looking forward,
Pretending not to notice,
I was a Opossum,
Country girl from The South,
With a swamp bottom,
Hips that could spread across Africa,
A smile that stretches across the Universe,
And yet,
You managed to make me small with your infidelities,
No matter how beautiful I was,
You would still take her call,
At a table I made a seat for you,
A meal prepared by my hands,
I played dead,
Pretended that I still loved you as I once did,
But I wasn't filled,
I was hollow,
My belly fed,
My soul hungry for you...

WAS

Why wasn't I enough,
Was my ass too soft,
And my heart too tough,
Hardened by hard heads,
That did too much,
I was as complete as I could be,
Reaching for you,
While searching for me,
But I couldn't hold us both,
My heavy heart,
And your lies,
I couldn't tote,
I did the best I could do,
Still wondering,
Why wasn't I enough for you,
Why wasn't I enough,
We're my kisses too soft,
And my eyes too tough,
Piercing through what I thought was deceit,
What falsehoods I imagined you'd be telling me,
My ears couldn't take it,
But my mind manipulated,
Your "maybe's" into truth,
Your roaming into couth,
Your ill intent into "he'll do",
Knowing that you won't do,
What I needed from you,
But this tethering had me questioning,

Why wasn't I enough,
Was my pussy too wet,
And my words too tough,
Making heavy out of light,
Your nightly deeds,
In mornings light,
Through yonder window breaks,
My heart into a thousand Shakes,
I did the best that I could do,
A sonnet of my love for you,
An orange moon,
Cratered with holes,
In her highs and her lows,
The tide will change,
I will silence your existence,
And never speak thine name,
And distance myself from the shame,
Of ever thinking I wasn't enough,
When the truth is,
I was always too much,
My ass is too soft,
My heart should be tough,
My kisses are fluff,
My eyes never lie,
Like my honest soul,
Who almost drowned in tears I've cried,
I've had to pick myself up,
And realize that you were never enough...

LET THEM EAT CAKE

You can have your cake and eat it, too, but not in my kitchen.

TO MY EX(x)

You can't say that you're in love with me and serve yourself... you're worshipping the wrong God.

THE MORNING AFTER

I looked at myself in your bathroom mirror,
The en suite just inches from your bed,
And I wondered,
How many women have arranged themselves in
This looking glass,
Slicked back their short styles,
Combed out their long weaves,
Braided in their faux twists,
Or pulled out their Afros,
Like me,
Brushed their teeth before your eyes part,
So that their morning kisses could be sweet,
As darkness turns to dawn,
Pinch their nipples so that they could be hard and perky,
Under lingerie that makes them uncomfortable,
When they prefer their naked warm bodies,
Against cool satin sheets,
Blown softly by an oscillating fan,
I wondered how many times,
They peaked from the door,
Making sure that they would be a surprise,
Making sure to always be perfect for you,
The one with crust in his eyes,
Dried drool around his lips,
Boogers in his nose,
A wet one hanging from a long hair that should be trimmed,
We went to bed strangers,
And woke up even stranger,
But I looked in that mirror and accepted that,
I accepted your ashy feet,
Over my perfect body smoothed in Moroccan oil,
I accepted your must-stained tee shirt,

Over my French lace and nude pumps,
Come on,
Everybody loves a nude pump,
Even when they don't love you,
I accepted that too,
You were my favorite stranger,
Living,
For the lie of you,
I'm my favorite stranger too,
Not knowing who the woman is in the speculum
Before me,
Could be my twin,
She resembles all of my features,
She has my same questions,
Same bewilderment,
We wonder,
How many women have arranged themselves in
This looking glass,
And how much longer will we be strangers...

THE MAN I CAN'T TASTE

I remember that day I kissed you,
And felt nothing,
Your lips were so technical after you laid with her,
Two fleshy lines,
Pressed up against mine,
But nothing spectacular,
Nothing terrific,
Just your lying lips,
Against my trying lips,
A heart that tried to love you through betrayal,
A mind that tried to make reason of your faults,
A wound,
Packed with salt,
Open,
Reaching for your healing balm,
For your open arms,
But nothing happened,
A plain kiss,
The stench of her lust on your fingers,
Don't touch me anymore,
I can't look at you,
I tried,
I saw nothing,
I cried,
You did nothing,

I remember that day,
You shattered my soul,
And tried to mend in with your sorry, empty kisses,
Apologetic only for being caught,
Don't kiss me,
I don't taste kisses that aren't real,
Don't love men that aren't real,
You were a fantasy,
Turned into memories,
Somebody that I used to know,
If people ask,
"Nah, I don't know him no more".

ONCE AGAIN

We fell into that comfortable place,
Between boxer briefs and black lace,
Because I'm easy,
And you're easy,
Even when it's hard...

YOUR HONEY AIN'T SWEET

I wish I could break you into all of the pieces you left me in,
I wish I could see you scatter and fall into nothingness,
I wish your smile gets lost in an ocean of tears,
Your words muffled under hands that can not separate from your lips,
I hate you,
It's true,
Because I once loved you more than the moon,
You were my sun,
I carried your seed,
Now,
I only wish to see you in shambles,
The way I look every time you see me,
The way I crumbled when you left me,
I wish all of your questions stay unanswered,
I wish someone uses you the way you used me,
Leave you lonely and empty,
Leave you bitter before you get better,
If better ever comes,
I hope it doesn't,
So that you can row your boat down a stream,
So dark and tainted from my dreams,
I wish your dreams never come true,
And I haunt your thoughts for all time,
All of that time is mine,
Subtracting what's due,

You took from me,
I take from you,
I wish you knew what it's like,
To drown in your sorrows at night,
Can't sleep,
Eyes tote luggage,
Anger tugging at your soul,
This is shit hurts,
I wish you feel it forever,
So next time you decide,
To skin your lover alive,
You'll think twice...

SHOULDA, COULDA, WOULDA

I shoulda cussed yo ass out,
The first time you showed up late at my house,
Or the first time you told me that you were meeting with her,
I had all kinds of words lodged in the back of my throat,
All the bad things I wanted to say,
But I choked,
On yo sorry ass "I love you",
Hell,
I shoulda cussed my ass out,
For believing anything that came out of your mouth,
I remember the first lie you told,
But my hands you would hold,
And lies became truth,
And I became you,
Still making love to someone who didn't respect my mind,
I shoulda cussed yo ass out for wasting my time,
Taking my tender youth,
And turning it into,
Lessons close to middle age,
All the things I learned past my college days,
That I guess I never learned,
You still snuck in and burned,
Holes in my heart,
And my rugs,
You smoke damn too much,
I shoulda cussed yo ass out,
For stinking up my house,
Smelling like Swisher Sweets, corn, and old feet,
Toes that need clipping,
Tearing up my damn sheets,

And now I'm cold,
You entertaining women,
And there's no one in my bed to hold,
I shoulda cussed yo ass out,
For leaving me alone,
Even when you came back,
You made my door revolve,
Like a gun,
Like the one I shoulda shot when I saw you with her,
Killing ain't my style,
But making you think I would,
Would be worth my while,
Because you think I'm playing with yo ass,
Every time I took you back,
Because "I love you" was enough for me,
"I miss you" made me melt in between those sliced up sheets,
The way you whispered my name,
When your... average... rod was inside of my frame,
I could only picture you,
I shoulda cussed yo ass for not making my dreams come true,
You promised me,
A home,
A ring,
Babies,
Everything,
But it turns out you were the biggest lie,
I shoulda cussed yo ass out for making my cry,
All the tears I've cried,
I could water Mars,
I'm a shining star,
And you're just the dull ass fool who tried to break me,
Rearrange me,
Disarm my charm,

And put it in your pocket,
Locked me in,
With your fingers in my coils,
I shoulda cussed yo ass out when you said you wanted more,
I gave you everything I had,
But now I see,
You'll never be the man for me,
So I didn't waste my words,
On such a pawn, a peasant, a bird,
Fly away,
Be peace,
And leave my life,
I always love you....

No, wait, wait, wait, wait, wait...

Before you go you swamp gator mouth, fucking rat bitches with dry pussy and eating off brand cereal, no rhythm, can't fuck a hole in a paper bag, Ohio river seeking, auction block, bought and paid for raggedy ass motherfucking negro, two stepping in the name of fake ass thugs, hair thinning, gut growing, ass sniffing, garbage mouth lying, hoe chasing, cum-to-soon, sorry ass sap sucker...

Fuck you.

I shoulda cussed yo ass out sooner...

Bitch.

NOW THAT I HAVE YOUR ATTENTION
(THE LAST SAD POEM I WILL WRITE ABOUT YOU/POOF/HE GONE)

I was your captive audience,
Turned captured wench,
Chained beside you,
Your sweet nothings,
Became sour nothings,
And made my ears bleed,
Bought and sold,
Separated from days of old,
Then time smashed us together,
Fleshly bodies crashed into each other,
And you told me, "it was nothing",
How can I be nothing when I'm something,
You had me questioning my existence,
Crying every time I listened,
To a song that reminded me of you,
I stopped listening,
And became an island,
A fleshy mass,
Floating on my tears,
The years became waves,
That crashed into my side,
Kept me up at night,
I'm sure you slept,
I'm sure you slept with her,
I had a dream there was a duffle bag full of panties under your bed,

My size,
But not my style,
I found mascara in your bathroom,
So I threw the tube at your head,
While you slept,
But it was just a dream,
And granny told me, "let sleeping dogs lie",
Because dogs with open eyes will always tell you lies,
And their tail won't tuck between their legs,
It will wag,
Furiously,
They will brag,
Famously,
About how you took a stray in,
And made him kin,
And he just made you nothing...

CALM.

Calm is a weeping willow that weeps less and allows the wind to breeze through spaces that long for healing.

MISCARRIAGE

My love, I just want to carry you.

A QUILTED COOL OF CONNECTION

I want to stitch my pain to you,
And make a tapestry of our togetherness,
We would be less ugly together,
Let me mend that broken place in you,
And cut off the part of me that died,
Sew the edges of myself to yourself,
We could be a new self,
A quilted cool of connection,
I want the pieces of you that you think don't matter,
Black pain matters,
Black healing matters,
Black art matters,
Let me hang you on my walls,
All of them,
I love you,
You're a puzzle I never finish,
Just work on when I can,
Let me work on you,
Over and over,
I'll never figure you out,
But I don't want to,
I want to stitch,
That itch that you can't scratch,
My needle can puncture that,
Hopelessness,
Let me hope for you,
Turn you into a blanket that we wrap around our child,
Cover her in our threads,
She looks like a complete picture of us,
Born into her fullness,
We made her whole,

Out of Black pain spun into gold,
I want to stitch my love to you,
Keep you together when your fabric frays,
This time,
I'll make us into a curtain,
Hang us in a window and let the sunlight shine through us,
I love you,
You look glorious in the light,
You look like an eclipse on the darkest night,
With one bright star in your eye,
Let me cry for you,
Keep your moons free from tears,
Black glow matters,
Black stars matter,
Black babies matter,
Let's make more perfect children,
And free our people,
A quilted cool of connection,
From the ancestors to the ether,
The here and now and beyond,
I love you,
Let me love you through me loving me,
I will keep you,
Stitch you close,
Stitch you tight,
We are one,
Forever.

HIDE AND SEEK

I hid you in my cervix,
On that spot that always makes me cum,
So whenever I say your name,
My body knows how to respond.

QUESTION

"Why do I still love him?",
I ask myself daily,
He's given me many so reasons to not love him so,
He's given me so much heartache,
I'll never know,
If I'll be whole again,
Wondering,
"When can I loose myself from him?",
I ask myself daily,
Like a prayer,
I ask for mercy,
On my sweet forgiving soul,
I ask to let him go,
And for Goddess to let me be,
Into myself,
Love him less,
Love me more,
Close the door to his potential,
And open the windows to air him out,
He smells of her,
And her,
And her,
And her,
And her as well,
I didn't deserve this Hell,
To smell another woman on my man,
For my hand to be empty,
Not holding his hand,
"Why do I still love him?",
I ask myself daily,
He's given me so many reasons not to love him so,

But back and forth we go,
Sea sick,
Rocking this ship,
Relationship,
Situation-ship,
Shipwrecked on the island of uncertainty,
"But he loves me,
Especially,
Different,
Every time we",
Fall into this trap,
Somewhere between a lie and the truth,
Somewhere between the old and the new,
And I fall,
For his eyes,
I fall for his lies,
I'm foolish,
I fall every time,
And I die daily,
Asking the same questions,
That always respond with,
"Maybe",
Maybe he loves me,
Maybe I still love him because,
Loving him was enough,
To make it through the day,
Even if I wasted away,
Into a canyon of nothingness,
But I don't want to waste,
I just want a taste,
Of what real love feels like,
I may never feel it again,
So why,
"Why do I still love him?"...

AN EVENING IN MISSOULA

An evening in Missoula,
With your hair covering my face,
You smell like Redwoods,
And fire,
I am alive with you,
Your kisses taste like morning dew,
Even when I'm mourning over you,
The love I lost and found again,
The man who evades me,
Escapes me,
And yet,
We end up here,
Over a glass of wine,
Or beer,
Over a thousand tears,
On this evening in Missoula,
I wish I knew a doula,
Who could birth this pain out of me,
And replace my womb with ecstasy,
On that spot you used to hit,
Long and deep,
And slow,
And seep,
Into every inch of my being,
I love you,
Even when you make my stomach turn,
Because it turns for you,
My heart burns for you,
This fire,
Lighting every tree in the forest ablaze,
It burns,
And It churns,
On this evening in Missoula...

YOU

It's something cosmic,
And something toxic,
That draws me to you,
I can't quit you,
Can't stop being your fool,
I wanna be your lover,
I love figuring out how to love you,
How to love myself when you leave me,
You will leave me,
However, you always come back,
I always take you back,
With you lineage on my back,
Tracing all the way back,
To Africa,
Warm like the sun,
Our people,
Dancing on the slick of my skin,
I take all of you in,
Can't figure why I can't quit you,
Your eyes,
Shaped like half moons,
Light my face,
With amazing grace,
I see you,
I don't always like what I see,
But I want to,
I want to want you,
My eyes beg for your forgiveness,
Free me,
I live for your pardon,
Your love is purgatory,

No heaven,
No hell,
Just the in between of my empty shell,
Filled with your cosmic dust,
Filled with your toxic smut,
Lungs filled with soot,
Your eternal blackness,
Your lack to love me,
Properly,
You only love me on occasion,
When it suits you,
When the next woman loots your soul,
You use my love to mend those holes,
So I mend you,
Lend you my ears,
Cry for you my Jodeci tears,
I keep on keeping on for you,
Trying to break from this cosmic cell,
This toxic jail,
Of your situational affections.

GOOD.

Good is a temperate day with the sun blinking through the clouds.

APEX

Who knew how much I needed you?
Our friendship,
Our connection,
Separated for years,
However we've never left each other,
You've always been with me,
And I,
A part of you,
I've loved you then,
I love you now,
I love you more,
Than ever,
Forever,
Thank Goddess for the God in you,
For jazz and candlelight,
Under the cherry moon,
For thick hair,
From our mamas,
For love from our aunties,
Who never bore children,
But poured infinite love into our souls,
I'll never let our friendship go,
Who knew how much I needed you,
Needed to refuel,
Needed to be reminded that I'm loved,
Needed to know that my love is still valuable,
I value you,
Your genuine spirit,
Your beautiful soul,
Your gorgeous face,
Wow,
Who knew how much I needed you?
I surely know now...
Much,
And much more.

BOULDERS OF STRENGTH FOR THE FALLEN

I should've told you that I loved you then,
When we passed each other in the hall,
When our eyes got caught,
Fixed upon each other from across the room,
I laughed with you,
Shared books and stories,
You were important,
I should've told you then,
At tournaments,
Competing for our Old Gold,
That Old Black,
Magic were we,
Young were we,
Eternity,
I thought I had with you,
To tell you that I loved your eyes,
Your smile could melt a thousand cubes of ice,
You were a hero,
I should've told you then,
You were a great friend,
I should've told you then,
You gave me joy,
I should've told you then,
That you were more than my classmate,
More than a face in an endless sea of faces,
You were special,

Maybe I'll tell you on the other side,
We'll sip sangria with Kings,
We'll race,
On clouds across space,
We'll see everyone we've ever loved,
And tell them,
Right then and there,
How much we care,
I am a fool for not telling you sooner,
I will not make that mistake again,
And I will speak your name,
Craig,
Michael,
Bobby,
All of my brothers and sisters expired by time,
You will not be forgotten,
I should've told you that I loved you then...

TREVIÑO LULLABY

Sleep, dear Brother,
We didn't lose you,
You only needed to rest,
Find some peace for your soul,
Struggle no more,
Float on clouds,
Ride comets through the cosmos,
See things that you've never seen,
And have a piece of the peace,
You so desperately needed,
Sleep, dear Brother,
We didn't lose you,
Your blood runs through our veins,
But we miss looking at your face,
We miss being in your space,
Your smile,
We smiled the same smile,
We looked up to you,
And empathized with your pain,
Hurt no more,
Worry not,
We will never forget you,
Sleep, dear Brother,
We didn't lose you,
We are beginning to understand your truth,
You found your freedom,
Abound with no rules,
Be free, dear Brother,
And Rest In Peace.

I WILL SPEAK YOUR NAME, YOU WILL NEVER DIE

Countless names of my people,
Who sat at the kitchen table with me,
Ate collard, and mustard, and turnip greens,
Ham with a slice of pound cake,
Breathing love,
In and out of their bodies,
Speaking of harder times,
Even in their speech those were "the good ole days",
For those were the days when change was fresh,
Revolution was in its infancy,
And hope was ever present,
I knew this for I sat at that table with them,
I was their hope,
I was their dream of a better day,
I was the recipient of their legacy,
They spoke of Charles Hamilton Houston,
They spoke of Sojourner's truth,
A beacon of light,
For our peoples plight,
I sat at their feet,
Looked in their eyes,
Listened to their stories,
And knew that my path would be the same,
I would be on a list of names,
Linked in a linage,
Whether by blood or association,
That will be etched into forever,

My body is a placeholder for my greatness,
My essence shall linger,
My life will be more than a vapor,
So in the spirit of them,
Those who bandaged my wounds when I fell off of a bike,
Those who tucked me in at night,
Those who gave me songs to sing,
And those that gave me this news to bring,
It is good news,
I will speak their names,
Their essence will leap from my tongue every chance I get,
Their stories will echo through time from my voice,
And the voices of my children,
Their photographs will be shared over hot tea and whiskey,
Their songs will be sung at protest,
Or while I lull my baby into The Land of Nod,
They, the giants on which I stand, will not be forgotten,
I will speak their names,
They will never die.

BAD.

Bad is a bitch on wheels with no brakes.

BLESSED BE

My loyalty is a blessing,
And I don't have to bless you,
Not even if you sneeze...

ALLEY OF WIND

The sky was screaming,
She was angry,
Unleashed,
Played the limbs of trees like puppets,
Loosened them with her tears,
Leaves blew,
Tumbled across the grass and pavement,
Tattered with holes from pebbles,
Dying from the separation,
Of the arms,
Waving Mahalia hallelujahs,
Thank you,
I say thank you oh sky,
For reminding me of your fury,
Wind hollers for help,
This way,
That way she turns,
Funnels into panic,
But her eye is calm,
Watching peacefully what destruction brings,
Splitting lumber and tossing brick,
The sky was screaming,
Throwing bolts of thunder,
Darting at our safe houses,
Rumbling the Earth about us,
I couldn't even be frightened,
I have seen her angrier,
I lay still as her screams echo in my head,
I don't move,
I listen,
Are freight trains near,
I question,

But I do not fear,
For I live in,
An alley of wind,
That tangos with city blocks,
Knocks power from its pedestal,
Clouds roll into darkness,
Morph into sheets of rain,
Barricade the light of stars,
Slap water against windows,
Scream on,
Screamer,
Til your screams come true,
A path of nothing,
Piles of memories,
Arranged in rubble,
Lit by the terror that flashes across the sky,
She is unhinged,
Raining a reign of vexation,
When her war cry shrieks,
Piercing the atmosphere,
I believe her motives,
Intentions to conjure Hell,
I listen,
And lay still,
A symphony of the torrent,
Its melancholy melody,
A lullaby,
Of the sky,
Her expression,
Met with sirens,
She was still angry,
There was no end,
Only Technicolor rainbows of Oz,
Witches crushed beneath the brick,
And a little girl who dreamt of a home,
That she will never see again…

FIRE DANCES WITH THE MOON

The cinders wrapped soot around the stars,
Amber embers bellowing into the night atmosphere,
And the gray monster of smoke,
Choking the structure in flames,
Chased our bare feet,
To pavement covered curbs down our street,
The chill could not contain the Fahrenheit,
The fire was felt as it danced with the moon,
We watched her seduce wooden beams,
She weakened them until they fell to Earth,
Nothing could stand in her presence,
Even windows bowed,
Blown out from the pressure of her persistence,
Fire,
Once shapeless in her moves,
Mimicked the house's frame,
Curved around the roof,
Seared the brick,
Burned the beams,
And let her charms rise to the sky,
Sky high she danced with the moon,
And we,
Bare footed and cold,
Watched her,
Our moans became her music,
But we had no song,

Our cries syncopated with sirens,
Our screams were rhythm-less,
Water interrupted her dance,
Smothered her smoke,
Scattered her soot,
Amber embers turned cold,
And smoke disappeared,
Toes attached to feet crept closer,
Our music hushed in corners of our mouths,
Whispers on our tongues,
Then silence fell where our hearts dwelled,
And now that fire danced in Hell...

I AM MY OWN MOTHER NOW

I am my own mother now,
Licking wounds and stitching scars,
Lacerations on my heart,
Sliced open and dug deeper,
By the woman who used to rock me to sleep,
But now she throws stones at my glass house,
Tries to break what she doesn't understand,
Cusses instead of comforts,
Rather see me on the streets,
Than see me near the stars,
And I never understood,
How somebody could,
Be so cruel,
From the body in which I suckled myself into the Land of Nod,
Gave me oil from the livers of cod,
To keep the cold at bay,
Then one day,
She changed,
Didn't love me the same,
Detested the sound of my name,
Scraped my soul,
Across her blackened coals,
And called it "love",
In the name of "cause I'm your mother",
But abuse in any form,
I can not tolerate to receive,
I had babies inside of me,
Little bodies,
Connected to my body,
That trauma connected to their cords,

I don't want that anymore,
For the sake of them,
I lost them all,
They couldn't swim in the toxic film,
Of our linage,
A kinship broken,
When she first punched me in my face,
Banged on my door,
Lied to my friends,
Threatened my life,
Negative cloud,
Of maternal rain,
I had to free myself,
From her Hell,
From her salt,
Always packed in my wounds,
Packed in my bags,
I've decided to unpack,
And be my own mother,
Brush my hair before I go to bed,
Sing songs to soothe my soul,
Make breakfast before a big day,
Paint my toes,
Write myself notes,
Be the mother I always wanted,
For myself,
For my babies,
They'll come back one day,
Push their way through my body,
And we'll all be healed,
I'll rock them to sleep,
Let them suckle until their tummies are round and full,
Smile at them,
Let them know a child,
Deserves their mother's smile,
Until that day,
I am my own mother now.

?

Why did I keep changing myself for you when you didn't love me in the first place? You sure as hell ain't gonna love someone we both don't know...

THE WINTER OF MY DISCONTENT

After a long night of quiet,
He went to work like he always did,
Left me in the bed half naked,
Half confused,
"Does he love me?",
I wondered,
Even though he held me all night,
His thoughts were clearly not in our room,
Our bodies warm,
Our bed cold,
Our lips sealed,
Quiet was essential,
So we went to sleep like we always did,
Held each other in question,
The morning brings only sun,
No answers,
He went to work like he always did,
And I was alone like I had always been...

CONDOMS AND DAMNATION

I took a lover for granted,
Made him wear two condoms,
Before he put it in,
I didn't want babies,
That's not true,
I didn't want babies with him,
It was the first time,
I let my mind be free,
Try this "physical" thing,
But it wasn't working,
I wouldn't call him,
Didn't think about him throughout the day,
My thoughts were fixed,
On this slick can of slick,
Another man who had vexed my soul,
This old lover had taken ahold,
Of my mind,
This new lover was a waste of time,
But I fucked him anyway,
Tried to fuck my pain away,
Tried to kiss my pain away,
Tried to sweat my pain away,
And capture his DNA in plastic,
So I could wrap it,
And trash it,
No traces of the night before,
Washed my sheets,
Sat in the tub for hours,
Saw the reflection of my old love,
In the water,

Damn him for being this strong,
My wrong could not erase his wrong,
And yet I longed for his touch,
His sweet open kisses on my hips,
His hands grabbing whatever part was within reach,
I ached for his sheets,
To cover the small of my back and my legs,
Whenever I rode his horse in bed,
But I went to see,
Another man,
About another horse,
And rode that ride furiously,
Call me Furious Styles,
No Chippy D,
But this physical thing,
Wasn't my style,
Or worth my while,
Sitting up in my room,
Thinking of all the things I used to do with my old love,
An ancient grain of sand,
Always shifting and moving my world,
To bring my thoughts closer to him,
I took a lover for granted,
Had him filling holes,
That he couldn't fill,
Had him digging for treasure that he'd never find,
Had his hands on my waist,
When I'd grind,
But it was never the same,
As when my old love would call my name,
Whisper, "CC", so sweetly,
In my ear,

And when it's all over,
That's all I want to hear,
Him calling my name,
This slick can of slick,
Making slick sticky between my hips,
I can't believe I still love him,
I tried to fuck him away,
I tried to kiss him away,
I tried to sweat him away,
Cut off his spirit in my DNA,
So I could bind it,
And rewind it,
Figure out where we went wrong,
And how wrong lasted so long,
I can't see 'em coming down my eyes,
So I've got to make this poem cry,
I've got to make this poem try,
To make sense,
Of this foolishness,
Fucking to get over what I'm under,
His spell,
And his Hell,
Trapped in a well of my lamentations,
Wanting once again to fuse my body with my soul,
Stop taking my new lover for granted,
And loose myself from the old,
Slick can of slick,
Don't know if my heart can do it,
I don't know if I can go through it,
To not feel anything,
And let myself be lonely,

Cold,
At night with pillows stacked around my frame,
This game I play,
Pretending that he's there,
To have his hands stuck,
In my curly hair,
To have his kisses on my back,
His tongue on my neck,
Erotic and free,
He dominates me,
Like he dominates the world,
Fucking and sucking on this Arkansas girl,
He made me come,
But never to my senses,
This back and forth was senseless,
And it wasn't fair,
My new lover could never touch my hair,
Or kiss me there,
Or dream with me,
He was a mound of flesh,
Between Egyptian cotton sheets,
Helping me fuck my old love away,
But in my mind he stayed,
On the spot he stained,
A tad bit ugly around the edges,
My toes curl around the ledges,
Wanting to leap,
And live in the sky...

UGLY.

Ugly is a hard truth with piercing onyx eyes.

TIME IS A BIRD

Time is a bird,
Her wings shutter and flutter fly,
I sat in my favorite tree,
And plucked her,
Tried to make her less beautiful,
So the world wouldn't fuck her,
And leave her wondering,
Where did time go,
When she can't find her way home,
Or herself,
Hands dirty wind,
Red line becomes a slow grind,
And she watches herself,
Morph from a bird,
Into ash,
Burned from all the things she did for cash,
Swallowed worms for breakfast,
But she couldn't feed her kids,
Or her soul,
Time is a pile of cinders from days of old,
Waiting to emerge,
Somewhere in the deserts of Arizona,
Waiting for ash to once again be wings,
Longing for the ground to be a cloud,
Wanting to soar instead of whore,
Herself into a meager existence,
Because of her resistance to be free,
Time is mystery,
In a locked room,
A caged bird,
Behind bars too soon,

Her wings don't spread,
Only her legs,
Under full moons,
But she's an orange moon,
In a black hole,
With decomposing fools,
I tried to save her from herself,
I know that life all too well,
I travel time,
On his lap I dirty wind,
Waiting for him to set me free,
He doesn't have those keys,
Doubt is a chain,
That wraps around courage,
Only to discourage you from taking flight,
Remember the time,
When time was a bird,
How lovely she was,
Before she was plucked and fucked,
I helped her sew back on her wings,
And oh,
The places we can go,
When ash morphs into feathers,
So she and I stuck together,
And made a life on our own terms,
Once again,
That faithful day did not pass us by,
Time is a bird,
And we're supa dupa fly.

SEEDS AND WHATNOTS

His suns and daughters all had moons for eyes,
Little chocolate babies with ham hock thighs,
So precious and curious and sweet,
From their hair on their head,
To the toes on their feet,
I couldn't deny them,
But this also meant I couldn't try with him,
To have suns with moons,
Or daughters in bloom,
Or jumping a broom,
I made,
Out of straw and twine scented of coconut wine,
My body couldn't take it,
Being yet another greenhouse for his seeds,
Seeds sown in gardens unknown,
I want to know,
But how will I know if he really loves me,
If these suns and daughters,
Who all have moons for eyes,
Are always sprouting as a new surprise,
He has babies,
Little chocolate babies with ham hock thighs,
He made a brighter light,
Between their mothers' thighs late one night,
There was sweating,
And moaning,
And groaning,
Love made with understanding,
I'm sure he was gentle,
Those evenings when,
His stars shot across their Universe,

And they made kin,
Kin and skin scraped off of sin,
And sight,
But their eyes were closed tight,
When they both came,
Then their child came,
New fruit from a new tree,
Don't pluck,
Don't take her heart after you fuck,
It's too raw and tender,
Her thighs turned into air benders,
To push forth his child,
His suns and daughters all had moons for eyes,
Little chocolate babies with ham hock thighs,
So precious and curious and sweet,
From their hair on their head,
To the toes on their feet,
I couldn't deny them,
But this also meant I couldn't try with him,
To have suns with moons,
Or daughters in bloom,
Or jumping a broom,
I made,
Out of straw and twine scented of coconut wine,
My body couldn't take it,
Being yet another greenhouse for his seeds...

ONCE UPON A TIME

We were sisters once,
Held hands and cried over our ex-lovers,
In each other's laps,
Shared stories and secrets,
Made food together,
Combed each other's hair,
Scratched out those hard places,
And made them soft again,
She understood my heart,
Never let me fall,
Then something happened that changed that all,
We are strangers now,
Barely speak,
Exchange pseudo-pleasantries
if we see each other on the street,
Maybe we hug,
But we don't know each other now,
Don't share secrets,
Or food,
We don't cry,
We can hardly look at each other in our eyes,
It's awkward,
Because I love her,
We were sisters once,
And I miss her everyday...

HIM

He was a veil of sadness that couldn't be lifted,
Fabric morphed into stone,
And all my eyes knew was his darkness,
I couldn't see my own light,
My own might,
To free myself from this Hell.

REMINDING MYSELF THAT IT TAKES TIME

I was finally doing okay without you,
I sat in the floor for days,
Pulled apart the knots that you left in my stomach,
Carefully threading through,
And trying to undo the hurt that you caused,
I cried some,
Remembered when I wasn't knotted so,
When I would smile at the sound of your name,
How my heart would skip a beat,
Then flutter like a butterfly,
Those wings have since been clipped,
I don't fly like I used to,
Get high at the thought of you,
I began to get sick,
My eyes became clouds,
Always water falling from those skies,
Loving you was like pouring into a glass with holes in it,
Empty and knotted,
I didn't spot it,
Until I saw who you really were,
A tyrant with a dick,
A slick can of oil with slippery lips,
Slippery when wet,
When your tongue licked against my Black Pyramid,
When your lips became my lips,
And I made sense of your lies,
I would spend my nights making excuses for you,
My auntie told me,
"Never make excuses for a man",

But I did,
With tears in my lids,
So on this floor I sit,
Pulling apart the knots that you left in my stomach,
Miles of hurt,
Tangled,
Torturing my soul,
Even as I let you go,
I miss you,
Wanting to make peace,
And make believe,
That one day you'll be good for me,
You'll see how wonderful and glorious I am,
And turn knots back into butterflies,
But you're not magic anymore,
Just a man who left me sitting on the floor,
Pulling knots out of my stomach...

IN AND OUT OF LOVE

On this wave of your beautiful,
In a lull of your ugliness,
I ride through it all.

(DIS)CARD

I longed to be your favorite poem,
Dreamt that you would place me between your palms,
Read me,
See me,
But you used your hands to ball me up,
And throw me away,
Crumbled in a basket of your discards,
With rotting meat and used condoms,
I struggled to unfold myself,
Your trash is not my truth,
Truth is,
I am my favorite poem,
My coconut oiled palms salve over my wounded spaces,
My warm tears steam and straighten wrinkled places,
I stretched myself out,
And became tall again,
After your rejection shrank me in a way I have yet to recover from,
I love you still,
Even though I swallowed your jagged little pill,
However I long for you no more,
I write my name three times on the sleeve of my shirt,
I haven't thought of you,
Until just now,
Even that thought is fleeting,
Who knew you were once so strong,

That you could break my spirit and my heart at the same time,
A lifetime ago,
But today I remember I am not bagged trash,
Reclaim my glory,
Smile with my teeth,
Arch my back,
Pull my hair closer to Goddess,
She said,
"Let there be light",
She made me,
I am light,
You're just a dim memory,
And my favorite poem lives on.

LOVELY.

Lovely is me.

YOU DON'T WANT TO FALL IN LOVE WITH ME

The duties of a Queen are great and they are many,
If you can't handle the Goddess within,
Don't give me diamonds or babies,
Don't give me rubies or roses,
I prefer companionship over coins,
You don't want to fall in love with me,
I'm not easy,
I'm empathic,
Sensitive to every vibration,
I cry too much,
I smile too much,
It's confusing,
There is comedy and tragedy without reason,
I miss my Daddy,
No one will ever compare,
My heart has been torn in shards of sharpness,
I forget that I am soft,
I'm always putting pieces together,
Fabric,
Plays,
And myself,
The Queen stays busy,
I help people often,
Even when I am without,
I love my mother,
However we don't always see things squarely,
I miss her,

I miss my old love,
He was the worst,
He was the best,
He was mine,
Now he's lost to time,
I think of him often,
And you can't stop me,
We had babies,
We lost babies,
I think of them often,
See,
I'm flawed,
But because I'm Queen,
People fawn over me,
Praise me for only what they see,
Always give me things because I'm beautiful,
However they never give me credit for the things I
think are ugly,
Don't give me things,
Don't give me excuses,
Don't tell me lies,
I live for the truth,
It makes my heart tick,
Truth makes my soul sing,
This is the secret of the Queen,
I have many secrets,
And all can be revealed at any time,
My spirit longs to be open,
I closed it off,
Too many trying to raid the temple,
Defile me with deceit,
I don't trust easily,

You don't want to fall in love with me,
I want too much,
I desire my needs to be met,
Warmly embraced with kindness,
People are cruel,
Don't be cruel,
It will break me yet again,
I'll have to start over yet again,
Circles and cycles,
Moons over valleys,
A wide world of myself,
Empty,
Making room for you,
Who ever you are,
Making room for me,
Eternally expanding,
Being Queen is hard,
It's also fun,
Mostly hard,
I think too much,
Don't sleep too much,
Working,
Always working,
Still in a hole,
Still trying to figure the figuring of things,
It doesn't always work,
But I love myself,
That matters much,

I still think of his love,
My Daddy,
My old love,
See,
You can't make me stop thinking of him,
Of them,
Of my babies,
I wish they were here,
All of them,
Queens need love outside of themselves,
Even when she turns herself into herself
and becomes herself,
She may need you,
I need you,
Whoever you are,
Wherever you are,
This is your warning,
You don't want to fall in love with me.

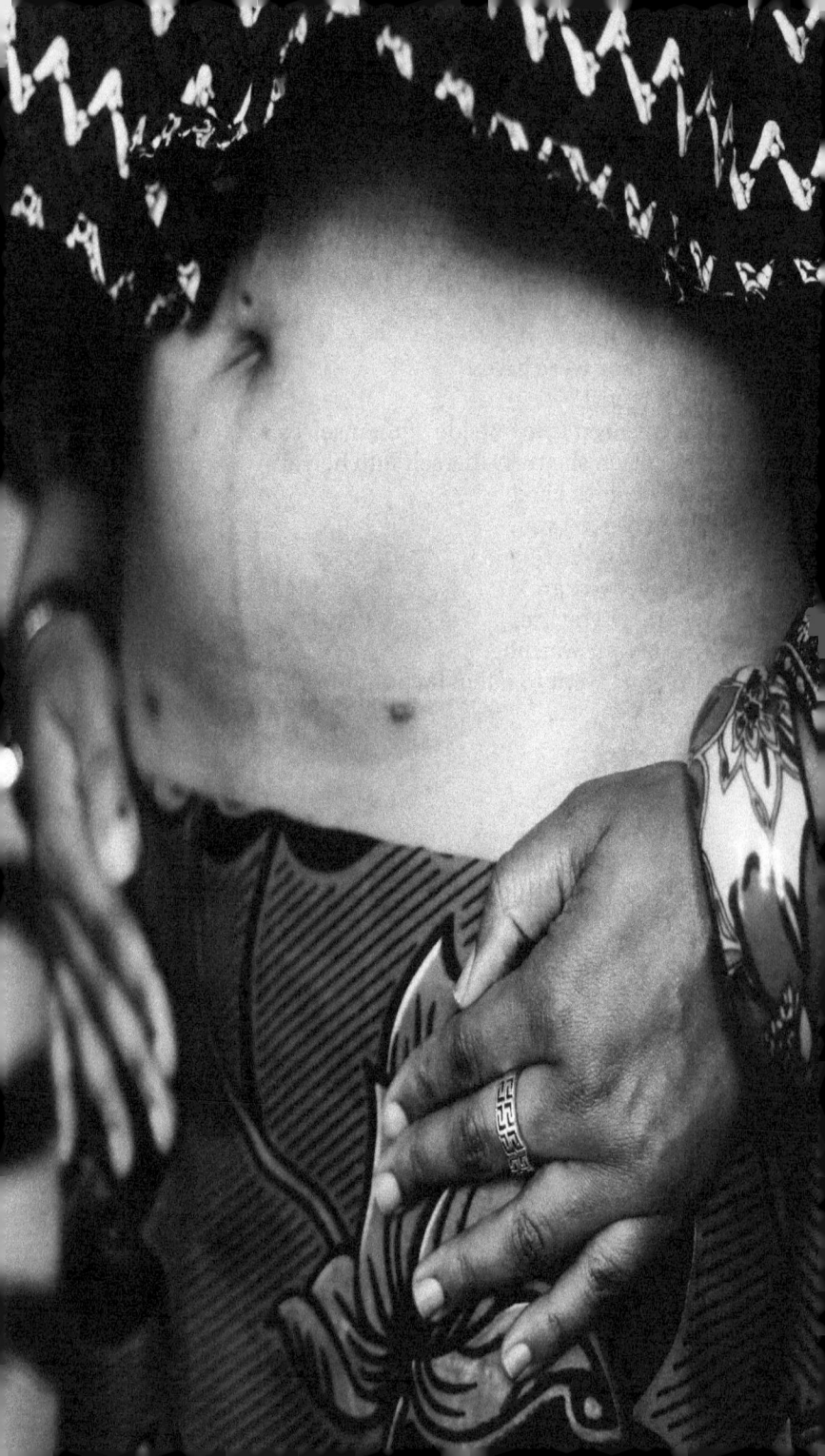

THAT TIME:
A LETTER TO MY WOMB

You twist,
And tangle,
And expand,
And contract,
To remind me,
That I am woman,
I love you,
Even when it hurts to love you,
The babies we've lost,
Can't find them,
Can't find the right man,
Worthy of entering your walls,
The crevices,
The crawl,
Spaces,
That lead to the knowledge of all,
But we don't look for him,
We just look to each other,
I hold you at night,
Dreaming about MerciPearl,
Rubbing cramps into dreams preferred,
Speaking softly,
Speaking sweetly,
I tell you,
I love you,
I mean it,
You are my world,
Together we've made new worlds,
We've made men come,
Made babies,

I'm sure they were beautiful,
Though they didn't survive,
We did,
We survived the knife,
Our first surgery at 22,
Our last at 33,
Hopefully,
No one will ever have to cut you open again,
To remove tumors, or cancers, or babies,
Let's keep the babies,
Let's not miscarry them,
Let's carry them carefully,
I'll stay off my feet,
If you hold them near until it's time to crown,
The future King or Queen of Blackness,
Let us teach them that their bodies are sacred,
Like a temple with text that only they would understand,
Let's teach them that their spaces are holy,
They are divine,
Even though that old pervert defiled
our temple that time when we were 15,
He is a rapist,
You are a Goddess,
My Goddess,
I love you,
Prayed you back into a healthy space,
You deserve it,
And even on this day,
When you mourn,
Phantom pains,
Pulling at your basket of eggs,
Gnawing on your tubes,
Scraping at the half of a cervix you have left,
I feel you,
We're hurting,
But let us be healed,

Everyday,
I tell you,
I love you,
I mean it,
You are my world,
I pray for your wholeness,
And our oneness,
You remind me,
That I am woman,
If I am woman,
You are the Universe,
Black and deep,
Your eggs are the stars that litter and glitter the sky,
The sun,
Rises and sets on your glory,
Dearest womb,
Work through this pain,
I promise,
We'll make it,
I love you,
Even when it hurts to love you...

I. AM. PERIOD.
A WORKING LIST

I am destructive.
I am griot.
I am sexy.
I am love.
I am keeper.
I am restorative.
I am heaven.
I am smooth.
I am intelligent.
I am flower.
I am tree.
I am grass.
I am crystal.
I am gem.
I am dust.
I am dawn.
I am lover.
I am power.
I am fearless.
I am hell.
I am fire.
I am black.
I am sky.
I am goddess.
I am mother.

I am baby.
I am woman.
I am sister.
I am friend.
I am cousin.
I am auntie.
I am patient.
I am rage.
I am ready.
I am water.
I am storm.
I am moon.
I am star.
I am local.
I am global.
I am universe.
I am poem.
I am sure.
I am evolving.
I am spell.
I am revolution.
I am angry.
I am calm.
I am changing.
I am everything.

SUGAR

You should know who I am,
Before you put your sugar on my yams,
Before you butter my buns,
With your spread or your jam,
This jelly won't shake,
And this ass won't quake,
Unless you take,
Your time,
Don't even think about taking my mine,
Wasting my years,
Shedding my tears,
Or heighten my fears,
To boost your ego,
This Black Pyramid,
Isn't accepting excuses,
So if you fall short,
You need not apply,
You must be this intelligent to ride this ride...

FRIDA'S INSTRUCTIONS

He thought I was magic,
That brown eyes,
And big yella thighs,
Could do anything,
That his legs between my knees,
Made him King,
And the arch in my back,
Made me Queen,
All hail to the Queen,
She smells like Egypt,
And wet clay,
She looks like yams,
Baked in midday,
All orange and golden delicious,
And her tongue was vicious,
Taking down heads,
Like a cyclone in her bed,
And he was mesmerized,
He thought I was magic,
That curly hair,
And lace underwear,
Could do anything,
That his mouth on my Black Pyramid,
Made him King,
And my ankles on his ears,
Made me Queen,
All hail to the Queen,
Her magic tastes like cabbage,
And turnip bottoms stewing in a pot,

Cornbread,
And an ice cold soda pop,
On a steamy summer's day,
Wasting the day away,
Under ruffled sheets,
Hip-Hop beats,
And poetry,
Gazing into each other's hearts,
He was in awe,
Cause,
He thought I was magic,
That big lips,
And wide hips,
Could do anything,
That his kisses on my neck,
Made him King,
And the moans in my throat,
Made me Queen,
All hail to the Queen,
She smells like a merchant of dreams,
And long days,
She looks like Black Power,
In a raspberry beret,
All royal and such,
And her truth was the realest,
That was the spell,
Good things are real,
And her magic was not for sale,
It was gift,
And he earned it,
Over sage prayers,
She burned it,
And made magic with him every night,
He thought I was magic...
And he thought right...

BLACK LOVE

Mother,
I am mother,
Cavern of Color,
Even though my womb,
Became a tomb,
I am still mother,
Ruff and tough with my Afro puffs,
Survived the ages with my Noire blood,
Black babies,
I am my mother's Black baby,
She is her mother's Black baby,
Going way back,
To the primordial ooze of Black,
Sun people,
Dark babies,
In all shades,
Let them suckle,
I am mother,
Highlight of Color,
Taken out of my father's arms,
Sold,
Captured,
Diluted,
Doesn't matter,
Still Black,
Black Lives Matter,
Black Babies Matter,
Black Love Matters,
Black History Matters,
For it is the history of the world,

Still mother,
Still lover,
Still here,
Smiling through my tears,
Healing,
Black bodies,
Making Black babies,
One day,
They will split the apex of the Black Pyramid,
Crown,
Wear their crown,
My mother's' paid for it ions ago,
I gladly pass it on,
That's love.

ABOUT THE BOOK

A LOVE STORY WAITING TO HAPPEN is a rhythmic, raw, and open movement of poetry that explores love, grief, mourning, freedom, social justice, sex, and courtships. The stunning black and white photography of Joshua Asante, lead singer of noted bands Amasa Hines and Velvet Kente, is the perfect pairing to C. C. Mercer's pain and progress in her poetry. His images compliment the stories that are being told, and they capture the essence of Mercer's confidence, vulnerability, femininity, boldness, and strength. Blending an intoxicating concoction of poetry and imagery, Mercer engages her intuitive intellect, molding herself to express stories that are both universal in nature and indicative of her journey in the full spectrum of love... Ebb. Flow. Disruption. Choas. Calm. Good. Bad. Ugly. Lovely.

ABOUT THE AUTHOR

CRYSTAL C. MERCER is a native of Little Rock, Arkansas. She's a Performance Artist, Poet, Activist and the Sole Proprietor of Columbus Creative Arts + Activism and SAFI FABric MARKET. Mercer's past credits include a number of plays and musicals in Arkansas, off - Broadway in New York, and internationally in Canterbury, England. Mercer fuses arts and activism by using theatre and textiles to tell social justice narratives, through merchandising and storytelling, with an emphasis of uplifting voices of color. A dedicated public servant, a woman of many creative talents, and daughter of the legendary late civil rights lawyer, Attorney Christopher C. Mercer, Jr., she honors the legacy of her father by using theatre arts as a tool for empowerment, education, and social justice. Stay connected to her: Crystal C. Mercer on YouTube, @colleenmercer on Instagram, @AfroCannGoddess on Twitter, @AfroGoddessCCM on Snapchat, @ccmercer on LinkedIn and @CCMercerToo on Facebook.

PHOTO INDEX

IN ORDER OF APPEARANCE. ALL PHOTO CREDITS JOSHUA ASANTE. NOTE THAT ALL PHOTOGRAPHS WITH A BLACK DRESS WERE IN A SERIES THAT EXPLORED A FRACTURED FAMILY RELATIONSHIP. ALL NUDE PHOTOGRAPHS WERE A RECLAMATION OF MY WOMANHOOD, BODY, LOVE, AND SELF.

FRONT COVER
FC "UNIVERSE"
"My body is beautiful and able" (Today's Mantra/Prayer, pg. 23). Fabric draped by Clarice Abdul-Bey, taken at Nancy Nolan Photography Studio, June 2017.

TABLE OF CONTENTS
8 "CELESTIAL"
"The sky was screaming" (Ally of Wind, pg. 109). Taken at the home of Joshua Asante, March 2017.

EBB
24 "MY SCARS ARE MY BEAUTY MARKS"
"She remembers everything" (There Are Different Ways To Make Love, pg. 25). Post surgery reflection, taken at the home of Joshua Asante, March 2017.

28 "MY FATHER'S WATCH"
"Time is a bird..." (Time is a Bird, pg. 124). The watch of my late father, Attorney Christopher C. Mercer, Jr. Taken at the home of Joshua Asante, August 2015.

PHOTO INDEX CONTINUED

FLOW
33 "WINDOW SEAT"
"I cried some, remembered when I wasn't knotted so..." (Reminding Myself That It Takes Time, pg. 132). Nude, and in my element, taken at the home of Joshua Asante, August 2015.

37 "THE BIGGER THE AFRO, THE CLOSER TO GODDESS"
"Goddess. Shell. Heaven. Hell." (Praise Goddess, pg. 27). Open field in the East End, Little Rock, AR, May 2016.

DISRUPTION
41 "CIVIL, LEFT"
"In the beginning there was darkness, we have always been here, and here we will remain..." (Yes, I'm Mad As Hell, pg. 59). Underpass in East End, Little Rock, AR, May 2016.

45 "I DARE YOU TO CROSS ME"
"I do not pledge allegiance to any flag, that considers color less than human" (No Allegiance, pg. 42). Street Tunnel, North Little Rock, AR, May 2016.

49 "THE LYNCHING OF A NEGRO"
"I can't breathe..." (Jive Turkeys, pg. 48). Open field in East End, Little Rock, AR, May 2016.

PHOTO INDEX CONTINUED

DISRUPTION CONTINUED
53 "CHANNELING TUBMAN"
"Wear your love on your sleeve, and eat three moons for dinner" (Love Is Magic, pg. 35). Open field in East End, Little Rock, AR, May 2016.

57 "TUNNEL VISION"
"The chill could not contain the Fahrenheit" (Fire Dances With The Moon, pg. 111). Street tunnel, North Little Rock, AR, May 2016.

60 "ANCESTOR"
"I just wanna enjoy my freedom..." (Fact Checker, pg. 63). Open field in the East End, Little Rock, AR, May 2016.

CHAOS
66 "WHEN SHE REFLECTS"
"How many women have arranged themselves in this looking glass..." (The Morning After, pg. 73). Taken inside of my home, Little Rock, AR, July 2016.

70 "GROOVE"
"I shoulda cussed yo ass out sooner..." (Shoulda, Coulda, Woulda, pg. 84). Taken at Nancy Nolan Photography Studio, June 2017.

75 "SIT FOR A SPELL"
"Bathe in the sun, take in the Earth in all her glory..." (Sunbathing, pg. 38). Taken at the home of Joshua Asante, August 2015.

PHOTO INDEX CONTINUED

CHAOS CONTINUED
81 "SUGAR MAMA"
"You should know who I am, before you put your sugar on my yams…" (Sugar, pg. 149). Quapaw Quarter United Methodist Church, Little Rock, AR, September 2016.

CALM
94 "IN EVERY TIME"
"I flow, and pool into my quietness" (There Are Different Ways To Make Love, pg. 26). Taken at the home of Joshua Asante, March 2017.

98 "THERE IS LIGHT AT THE END OF THE TUNNEL"
"You can't say that you're in love with me and serve yourself… you're worshipping the wrong God" (To My Ex(x), pg. 72). Street tunnel, North Little Rock, AR, May 2016.

GOOD
103 "CROWN CRESCENT MOON"
"On this wave of your beautiful…" (In And Out Of Love, pg. 134). Open field, College Station, AR, September 2016.

BAD
113 "REALLY?"
"I can't quit you, can't stop being your fool…" (You, pg. 96). Taken at the home of Joshua Asante, August 2015.

PHOTO INDEX CONTINUED

BAD CONTINUED

118 "FLOWERS + WEEDS"
"Being yet another greenhouse for his seeds..." (Seeds and Whatnots, pg. 127). Taken at the home of Joshua Asante, August 2015.

UGLY

126 "THE WORLD BEFORE HER"
"... a daily prayer, to the Goddess that expands my lungs with air..." (Praise Goddess, pg. 30). Taken at the home of Joshua Asante, August 2015.

131 "CRYSTAL POWERS"
"She made me, I am light" ((Dis)Card, pg. 136). Taken at the home of Joshua Asante, August 2015.

LOVELY

142 "CUT OPEN"
"Rubbing cramps into dreams preferred" (That Time: A Letter To My Womb, pg. 143). Post surgery, taken at the home of Joshua Asante, March 2017.

146 "THIRD EYE"
"I am sure" (I. Am. Period. A Working List, pg. 148). Open field, College Station, AR, September 2016.

150 "SPELLBOUND"
"He thought I was magic... and he thought right..." (Frida's Instructions, pg. 152). Street tunnel, North Little Rock, AR, May 2016.

PHOTO INDEX CONTINUED

LOVELY CONTINUED
155 "STAR GAZE"
"We would be less ugly together" (A Quilted Cool of Connection, pg. 89). Taken at the home of Joshua Asante, March 2017.

157 "HER HALVES MADE WHOLE"
"I have many secrets" (You Don't Want To Fall In Love With Me, pg. 139). Taken inside of my home, Little Rock, AR, July 2016.

BACK COVER
BC "ABUNDANCE"
"I am universe" (I. Am. Period. A Working List, pg. 148). Fabric draped by Clarice Abdul-Bey, taken at Nancy Nolan Photography Studio, June 2017.

Butterfly Typeface Publishing

Contact us for all your
publishing & writing needs!

Iris M. Williams
PO Box 56193
Little Rock AR 72215
501-823-0574

www.butterflytypeface.com
info@butterflytypeface.com

www.ingramcontent.com/pod-product-compliance
Lightning Source LLC
Chambersburg PA
CBHW060836190426
43197CB00040B/2653